NEW SAYINGS OF JESUS

AND

FRAGMENT OF A LOST GOSPEL

GRENFELL AND HUNT

NEW SAYINGS OF JESUS

EGYPT EXPLORATION FUND

GRAECO-ROMAN BRANCH

NEW SAYINGS OF JESUS

AND

FRAGMENT OF A LOST GOSPEL

FROM OXYRHYNCHUS

EDITED, WITH TRANSLATION AND COMMENTARY,

BY

BERNARD P. GRENFELL, D.Litt., M.A.

HON. LITT.D., DUBLIN ; HON. PH.D., KOENIGSBERG ; FELLOW OF QUEEN'S COLLEGE, OXFORD ; LUCY
WHARTON DREXEL GOLD MEDALLIST OF THE UNIVERSITY OF PENNSYLVANIA ;

AND

ARTHUR S. HUNT, D.Litt., M.A.

HON. PH.D., KOENIGSBERG ; FELLOW OF LINCOLN COLLEGE, OXFORD

WITH ONE PLATE

AND

THE TEXT OF THE 'LOGIA' DISCOVERED IN 1897

WIPF & STOCK · Eugene, Oregon

Wipf and Stock Publishers
199 W 8th Ave, Suite 3
Eugene, OR 97401

New Sayings of Jesus and Fragment of a Lost Gospel from Oxyrhynchus
By Grenfell, Bernard P. and Hunt, Arthur S.
ISBN 13: 978-1-60608-422-9
Publication date 12/30/2008
Previously published by Oxford University Press, 1904

PREFACE

THE present edition of the *New Sayings of Jesus* and *Fragment of a Lost Gospel* is printed with some alterations, principally by way of abridgement, from the forthcoming publication of the two texts in *The Oxyrhynchus Papyri*, Part IV, nos. **654** and **655**, where a fuller discussion of the more technical points will be given, as well as collotype reproductions of both fragments. The 'Logia' discovered in **1897** (ΛΟΓΙΑ ΙΗCΟΥ, *Sayings of our Lord*) are reprinted from the revised text and translation given in *The Oxyrhynchus Papyri*, Part I, no. **1**.

BERNARD P. GRENFELL.
ARTHUR S. HUNT.

OXFORD,
April 1904.

CONTENTS

I. NEW SAYINGS OF JESUS

(a) INTRODUCTION.

OUR first excavations in 1897 on the site of Oxyrhynchus, one of the chief cities of ancient Egypt, situated on the edge of· the western desert 120 miles south of Cairo, were rewarded by the discovery of a very large collection of Greek papyri dating from the first to the seventh century of the Christian era. Of the numerous theological and classical texts which were then brought to light, none aroused wider interest than a page from a book containing Sayings of Jesus and published by us under the title of ΛΟΓΙΑ ΙΗΣΟΥ, *Sayings of our Lord*. After an interval of six years, during which we were principally engaged in the search for documents of the first three centuries B. C. in the Fayûm, we returned in February 1903 to Oxyrhynchus, with a view to an exhaustive examination of what has been on the whole the richest site in Egypt for papyri. This process of clearing the numerous mounds on a large scale has already resulted in further important discoveries, but will necessarily be both long and costly in the case of a town which is more than a mile in length ; and after the termination of a third season's work there, the end is still far from being in sight.

By a curious stroke of good fortune our second excavations at Oxyrhynchus were, like the first, signalized by the discovery of a fragment of a collection of Sayings of Jesus. This consists of forty-two incomplete lines on the back of a survey-list of various pieces of land (see *Frontispiece*). The survey-list, which was written in a cursive hand of the end of the second or early part of the third century before the back of the papyrus came to be used, provides a *terminus a quo* for the writing on the other side. This, which is an upright informal uncial of medium size, we should assign to the middle or end

of the third century; a later date than A. D. 300 is most unlikely. The present text is therefore nearly contemporary with
the ' Logia ' papyrus discovered in 1897, which also belongs to
the third century, though probably to an earlier decade. In
its general style and arrangement the present series of Sayings
offers great resemblance to its predecessor. Here, as in the
earlier ' Logia,' the individual Sayings are introduced by the
formula ' Jesus saith,' and there is the same mingling of new
and familiar elements ; but the second series of Sayings is
remarkable for the presence of the introduction to the whole
collection (ll. 1–5), and another novelty is the fact that one·of
the Sayings (ll. 36 sqq.) is an answer to a question, the sub-
stance of which is reported (ll. 32–6). It is also noticeable
that while in the first series the Sayings had little if any con-
nection of thought with each other, in the second series the
first four at any rate are all concerned with the Kingdom of
Heaven. That the present text represents the beginning of a
collection which later on included the original ' Logia ' is very
probable ; this and the other general questions concerning the
papyrus are discussed on pp. 20–36.

Excluding the introduction, there are parts of five separate
Sayings. The single column of writing is complete at the top,
but broken at the bottom and also vertically, causing the loss
of the ends of lines throughout. From ll. 7–8, 15, 25, and 30,
which can be restored with certainty from extant parallel passages, it appears that the lacunae at the ends of lines range
from twelve to sixteen or at most eighteen letters, so that of
each line, as far as l. 33, approximately only half is preserved.
The introduction and the first and fourth Sayings admit of an
almost complete reconstruction which is nearly or quite con-
clusive, but in the second, third, and fifth, which are for the
most part entirely new, though the general sense may often be
caught, the restorations are, except in a few lines, rather
hazardous. The difficulties caused by the lacunae are en-
hanced by the carelessness of the scribe himself, who makes
several clerical errors; in two cases (ll. 19 and 25) words
which were at first omitted have been added by him over the
line.

(b) TEXT.

We proceed now to the text, giving first a transcription of the papyrus and then a reconstruction in modern form. Square brackets [ ] indicate a lacuna, round brackets ( ) the resolution of an abbreviation, angular brackets ⟨ ⟩ a mistaken omission in the original, braces { } a mistaken addition. Dots within brackets represent the approximate number of letters lost ; dots outside brackets indicate letters of which illegible traces remain. In the accompanying translation supplements which are not practically certain are enclosed in round brackets.

24·4 × 7·8 cm.

ΟΙ ΤΟΙΟΙ ΟΙ ΛΟΓΟΙ ΟΙ [
ΛΗϹΕΝ ΙΗ͞Ϲ Ο ΖΩΝ Κ[
ΚΑΙ ΘΩΜΑ ΚΑΙ ΕΙΠΕΝ [
ΑΝ ΤΩΝ ΛΟΓΩΝ ΤΟΥΤ[
5 ΟΥ ΜΗ ΓΕΥϹΗΤΑΙ ⟩— [
ΜΗ ΠΑΥϹΑϹΘΩ Ο ΖΗ[
ΕΥΡΗ ΚΑΙ ΟΤΑΝ ΕΥΡΗ [
ΒΗΘΕΙϹ ΒΑϹΙΛΕΥϹΗ ΚΑ[
ΗϹΕΤΑΙ ⟩— ΛΕΓΕΙ Ι[
10 ΟΙ ΕΛΚΟΝΤΕϹ ΗΜΑϹ [
Η ΒΑϹΙΛΕΙΑ ΕΝ ΟΥΡΑ[
ΤΑ ΠΕΤΕΙΝΑ ΤΟΥ ΟΥΡ[
ΤΙ ΫΠΟ ΤΗΝ ΓΗΝ ΕϹΤ[
ΟΙ ΪΧΘΥΕϹ ΤΗϹ ΘΑΛΑ[
15 ΤΕϹ ΫΜΑϹ ΚΑΙ Η ΒΑϹ[
ΕΝΤΟϹ ΫΜΩΝ [.]ϹΤΙ [
ΓΝΩ ΤΑΥΤΗΝ ΕΥΡΗ[
ΕΑΥΤΟΥϹ ΓΝΩϹΕϹΘΑΙ [
ΫΜΕΙϹ
ΕϹΤΕ ΤΟΥ ΠΑΤΡΟϹ ΤΟΥ Τ[
20 ΓΝΩϹΘΕ ΕΑΥΤΟΥϹ ΕΝ[
ΚΑΙ ΫΜΕΙϹ ΕϹΤΕ ΗΠΤΟ[

ΟΥΚ ΑΠΟΚΝΗϹΕΙ ΑΝΘ[
ΡΩΝ ΕΠΕΡΩΤΗϹΕ ΠΑ[
ΡΩΝ ΠΕΡΙ ΤΟΥ ΤΟΠΟΥ ΤΗ[
ΟΤΙ
25 ϹΕΤΕ ΠΟΛΛΟΙ ΕϹΟΝΤΑΙ Π[
ΟΙ ΕϹΧΑΤΟΙ ΠΡΩΤΟΙ ΚΑΙ [
ϹΙΝ   ΛΕΓΕΙ ΙΗ͞Ϲ ⟩— . [
ΘΕΝ ΤΗϹ ΟΨΕΩϹ ϹΟΥ ΚΑΙ [
ΑΠΟ ϹΟΥ ΑΠΟΚΑΛΥΦΗϹΕΤ[
30 ΤΙΝ ΚΡΥΠΤΟΝ Ο ΟΥ ΦΑΝΕ[
ΚΑΙ ΘΕΘΑΜΜΕΝΟΝ Ο Ο[

[. .]ΕΤΑΖΟΥϹΙΝ ΑΥΤΟΝ Ο[
[. .]ΓΟΥϹΙΝ ΠΩϹ ΝΗϹΤΕΥ[
[. . . .]ΜΕΘΑ ΚΑΙ ΠΩϹ [
35 [. . . . .]ΑΙ ΤΙ ΠΑΡΑΤΗΡΗϹ[
[. . . .]Ν ⟩— ΛΕΓΕΙ ΙΗ͞Ϲ[
[. . . . .]ΕΙΤΑΙ ΜΗ ΠΟΙΕΙΤ[
[. . . . .]ΗϹ ΑΛΗΘΕΙΑϹ ΑΝ[
[. . . . .]Ν Α[.]ΟΚΕΚΡ[
40 [. . . . .]ΚΑΡΙ[. .] ΕϹΤΙΝ [
[. . . . .]Ω ΕϹΤ[
[. . . . . : . . . .]ΙΝ[

·   ·   ·   ·   ·   ·   ·

(c) THE SAYINGS WITH TRANSLATIONS AND NOTES.

INTRODUCTION. ll. 1–5.

{οἱ} τοῖοι οἱ λόγοι οἱ [. . . . . οὓς ἐλά-
·λησεν Ἰη(σοῦ)ς ὁ ζῶν κ[ύριος? . . . .
καὶ Θωμᾷ καὶ εἶπεν [αὐτοῖς· πᾶς ὅστις
ἂν τῶν λόγων τούτ[ων ἀκούσῃ θανάτου
οὐ μὴ γεύσηται.

'These are the (wonderful?) words which Jesus the living (Lord) spake to . . . and Thomas, and he said unto (them), Every one that hearkens to these words shall never taste of death.'

The general sense of the introduction is clear, and most of the restorations are fairly certain. In l. 1 an adjective such as 'wonderful' is necessary after οἱ [. For 'shall never taste of death' cf. Matt. xvi. 28, Mark ix. 1, Luke ix. 27, and especially John viii. 52, 'If a man keep my word, he shall never taste of death.' In these passages of the Synoptists 'taste of death' simply means 'die' in the literal sense; but here no doubt, as in the passage in St. John, the phrase has the deeper and metaphorical meaning that those who obey Christ's words and attain to the kingdom, reach a state unaffected by the death of the body. The beginning of l. 1 requires some correction, οἱ τοῖοι οἱ λόγοι οἱ being extremely ugly. The corruption of οὗτοι into οἱ τοῖοι is not very likely, and since τοῖος is found in late prose writers for τοιόσδε, the simplest course is to omit the initial οἱ. The restoration of l. 2 presents the chief difficulty. κ[ύριος is very doubtful; κ[αί followed by e. g. ἀποθανών ('Jesus who liveth, though dead') is equally likely, and several of the possible supplements at the end of the line require a longer word than κ[ύριος to precede. Another dative before 'and to Thomas' is required, and three alternatives suggest themselves : — (1) a proper name, in which case Philip or Matthias is most likely to have been coupled with Thomas. Apocryphal Gospels assigned to Thomas, Philip, and Matthias are known, and in the

second or third century Gnostic work called *Pistis Sophia* 70–1
Philip, Thomas, and Matthias are associated as the recipients
of a special revelation; (2) a phrase such as 'to the other disciples' (so Dr. Bartlet, cf. l. 32 and John xx. 26 'his disciples
were within and Thomas with them'); (3) Ἰούδᾳ τῷ] καὶ Θωμᾷ,
suggested by Professor Lake, who compares the frequent occurrence of the double name 'Judas also called Thomas' in the
Acts of Thomas. The uncertainty attaching to the restoration
is the more unfortunate, since much depends on it. If we
adopt the first hypothesis, Thomas has only a secondary place;
but on either of the other two he occupies the chief position,
and this fact would obviously be of great importance in deciding
the origin of the Sayings.

There is a considerable resemblance between the scheme of
ll. 1–3, 'the words . . . which Jesus spake . . . and he said,'
and the formulae employed in introducing several of the ear-
liest citations of our Lord's Sayings, particularly First Epistle
of Clement 13 'especially remembering the words of the Lord
Jesus which he spake in his teaching . . . for thus he said,'
Acts xx. 35 'and to remember the words of the Lord Jesus
how he himself said.' Dr. Rendel Harris had already (*Contemp. Rev.* 1897, pp. 346–8) suggested that those formulae
were derived from the introduction of a primitive collection of
Sayings known to St. Paul, Clement of Rome, and Polycarp,
and this theory gains some support from the parallel afforded
by the introduction in the new Sayings.

FIRST SAYING. ll. 5–9.

5   [λέγει Ἰη(σοῦ)ς·
μὴ παυσάσθω ὁ ζη[τῶν . . . . ἕως ἂν
εὕρῃ καὶ ὅταν εὕρῃ [θαμβηθήσεται καὶ θαμ-
βηθεὶς βασιλεύσει κα[ὶ βασιλεύσας ἀναπα-
ήσεται.

'Jesus saith, Let not him who seeks . . . cease until he
finds, and when he finds he shall be astonished; astonished
he shall reach the kingdom, and having reached the kingdom he shall rest.'

The conclusion of this Saying is quoted from the Gospel according to the Hebrews by Clement of Alexandria (*Strom.* ii. 9. 45) 'as it is also written in the Gospel according to the Hebrews " He that wonders shall reach the kingdom, and having reached the kingdom he shall rest."' In *Strom.* v. 14. 96 Clement quotes the Saying in a fuller and obviously more accurate form which agrees almost exactly with the papyrus, but without stating his source : — 'He who seeks shall not cease until he finds, and when he finds he shall be astonished, and being astonished he shall reach the kingdom, and having reached the kingdom he shall rest.' The word after ζη[τῶν in l. 6, to which there is nothing corresponding in the Clement quotation, is very likely the object of 'seek,' perhaps τὴν ζωήν, i. e. (eternal) 'life.' The purpose to which Clement turns the passage from the Gospel according to the Hebrews is to support the Platonic view that the beginning of knowledge is wonder at external objects, but this interpretation is clearly far removed from the real meaning of the Saying.

The opening sentence 'Let not him who seeks . . . cease until he finds' is parallel to Matt. vi. 33 'But seek ye first the kingdom,' and vii. 7 'Seek and ye shall find'; cf. too the 2nd Logion 'Except ye fast to the world ye shall in no wise find the kingdom of God.' The idea of the necessity for strenuous effort in order to attain to the kingdom has also much in common with the 5th Logion ('Raise the stone and there thou shalt find me'). The precise meaning of 'astonished' in the second and third sentences, 'when he finds he shall be astonished; astonished he shall reach the kingdom,' has been a matter of dispute; but, as Professor Harnack has recently shown, the nearest parallel is Matt. xiii. 44 'The kingdom of Heaven is like unto a treasure hidden in the field, which a man found and hid; and in his joy he goeth and selleth all that he hath, and buyeth that field.' Astonishment therefore is to be interpreted as a sign not of fear but of joy; cf. the use of θάμβος for joyful astonishment in Luke v. 9 'He (sc. Peter) was amazed and all that were with him at the draught of the fishes.' With the clause 'astonished he shall reach the kingdom,' i. e. reign with the Messiah, cf. the promise to the disciples in Matt.

xix. 28 'Verily I say unto you that ye which have followed me
in the regeneration when the Son of Man shall sit on the throne
of his glory, ye also shall sit upon twelve thrones, judging the
twelve tribes of Israel.' For 'shall rest' cf. Matt. xi. 28–9
'I will give you rest . . . ye shall find rest unto your souls.'
Both the language and thought of this Saying thus have marked
parallels in the Gospels, and there are several references to it
in early Christian literature, the most notable being in the
Second Epistle of Clement v. 5 'The promise of Christ is great
and wonderful and rest in the kingdom to come and life eternal,' and in the *Acts of Thomas* (ed. Bonnet, p. 243) 'They
who worthily partake of the goods of that world have rest, and
in rest shall reign.' While the picturesque and forcible character of the Saying is undeniable, very different views have
been taken concerning the genuineness of it, as is the case with
most of the uncanonical Sayings ascribed to our Lord ; but the
tendency of recent criticism has been to assign it a very high
place among the Sayings which do not rest on the authority
of the Gospels, and Harnack accepts it as substantially a true
Saying of Jesus.

SECOND SAYING. ll. 9–21.

λέγει Ἰ[η(σοῦς· . . . . . . τίνες
10 οἱ ἕλκοντες ἡμᾶς [εἰς τὴν βασιλείαν εἰ
ἡ βασιλεία ἐν οὐρα[νῷ ἐστιν ; . . . .
τὰ πετεινὰ τοῦ οὐρ[ανοῦ καὶ τῶν θηρίων ὅ-
τι ὑπὸ τὴν γῆν ἐστ[ιν ἢ ἐπὶ τῆς γῆς καὶ
οἱ ἰχθύες τῆς θαλά[σσης οὗτοι οἱ ἕλκον-
15 τες ὑμᾶς, καὶ ἡ βασ[ιλεία τῶν οὐρανῶν
ἐντὸς ὑμῶν [ἐ]στι [καὶ ὅστις ἂν ἑαυτὸν
γνῷ ταύτην εὑρή[σει . . . .
ἑαυτοὺς γνώσεσθε [καὶ εἰδήσετε ὅτι υἱοὶ
ἔστε ὑμεῖς τοῦ πατρὸς τοῦ τ[. . . . .
20 γνώσ⟨εσ⟩θε ἑαυτοὺς ἐν[. . . . .
καὶ ὑμεῖς ἐστε ηπτο[. . . .

' Jesus saith, (Ye ask ? who are those) that draw us (to
the kingdom, if) the kingdom is in Heaven ? . . . the fowls

of the air, and all beasts that are under the earth or upon the earth, and the fishes of the sea, (these are they which draw) you, and the kingdom of Heaven is within you ; and whoever shall know himself shall find it. (Strive therefore ?) to know yourselves, and ye shall be aware that ye are the sons of the (almighty ?) Father ; (and ?) ye shall know that ye are in (the city of God ?), and ye are (the city ?).'

The reconstruction of this, the longest and most important of the Sayings, is extremely difficult. Beyond the supplements in l. 15, which are based on the parallel in Luke xvii. 21 with the substitution of 'kingdom of Heaven,' St. Matthew's phrase, for St. Luke's 'kingdom of God' which is too short for the lacuna, and those in ll. 12–3, 16, and 18, the general accuracy of which is guaranteed by the context, it is impossible to proceed without venturing into the region of pure conjecture. There seems to be no direct parallel to or trace of this Saying among the other non-canonical Sayings ascribed to our Lord, and the materials provided by ll. 10–12 — 'they that draw,' the kingdom of Heaven and the fowls of the air — are at first sight so disparate that the recovery of the connexion between them may seem a hopeless task. But though no restoration of ll. 9–14 can hope to be very convincing, we think that a fairly good case can be made out in favour of our general interpretation. The basis of it is the close parallelism which we have supposed to exist between l. 15 τες ὑμᾶς καὶ ἡ βασ[ιλεία τῶν οὐρανῶν and, on the other hand, l. 10 οἱ ἕλκοντες ἡμᾶς followed in l. 11 by ἡ βασιλεία ἐν οὐρα[νῷ, whereby we restore οἱ ἕλκον-] at the end of l. 14. If this be granted ll. 9–16 divide themselves naturally into two parallel halves at the lacuna in l. 11, ll. 9–10 corresponding to ll. 12–5, and l. 11 to ll. 15–6. How is this correspondence to be explained ? The simplest solution is to suppose that ll. 9–11 are a question to which ll. 12–6 form the answer ; hence we supply τίνες in l. 9 ; cf. the 5th Saying, which is an answer to a question. A difficulty then arises that we have 'draw us' in l. 10 but 'draw you' in ll. 14–5. This may be a mere accident due to the common confusion of ὑμεῖς and ἡμεῖς in papyri

of this period, and perhaps 'you' should be read in both cases.
But 'us' in l. 10 can be defended in two ways, by supposing
either that Jesus here lays stress rather on His human than
on His divine nature, and associates Himself with the disciples,
or that the question is put into the mouth of the disciples, i. e.
the word before 'who' was 'ye ask' or the like. There remains, however, the greatest crux of all, the meaning of 'draw.'
A favourable sense is here much more likely than the reverse;
cf. John vi. 44 'No man can come to me except the Father
which sent me draw him,' and xii. 32 'I will draw all men
unto myself.' A phrase such as 'to the kingdom' is required
to explain 'draw,' though even with this addition the use of
that word in such a context must be admitted to be difficult.
The idea in ll. 12–6 seems to be that the divine element in the
world begins in the lower stages of animal creation, and rises
to a higher stage in man, who has within him the kingdom of
Heaven; cf. Clement's discussion (*Strom*, v. 13) of Xeno-
crates' view that even irrational creatures possibly had some
notion of the Divine, and the curious sanctity of certain animals
in the various Apocryphal Acts, e. g. Thecla's baptized lion-
ess, Thomas's ass, Philip's leopard and kid buried at the door
of the church. The transition from the inward character of
the kingdom to the necessity for self-knowledge (ll. 16–21) is
natural. Since the kingdom is not an external manifestation
but an inward principle, men must know themselves in order
to attain to its realization. The old Greek proverb 'know
thyself' is thus given a fresh significance. Mr. Badham well
compares Clement, *Paedag*. iii. 1 'It is then, as it appears, the
greatest of all lessons to know one's self. For if a man knows
himself he will know God.' For 'sons,' which is required by
the context in l. 18, cf. e. g. Luke xx. 36 'they are . . . sons
of God.' At the end of l. 19 π can be read in place of τ: the
word is probably an adjective, possibly $\pi[\alpha\nu\tau\sigma\kappa\rho\acute{\alpha}\tau\sigma\rho\sigma s$. $\eta\pi\tau\sigma[$ in
l. 21 is very obscure, and it is tempting to read $\mathring{\eta}$ $\pi\{\tau\}\acute{o}[\lambda\iota s$,
with $\grave{\epsilon}\nu$ $[\tau\mathring{\eta}$ $\pi\acute{o}\lambda\epsilon\iota$ $\tauο\hat{\upsilon}$ $\theta\epsilon o\hat{\upsilon}$ in l. 20, as Professor Blass suggests,
comparing for the omission of $\mathring{o}\nu\tau\alpha s$ Mark vi. 20 $\epsilon\mathring{\iota}\delta\grave{\omega}s$ $\alpha\mathring{\upsilon}\tau\grave{o}\nu$
$\mathring{\alpha}\nu\delta\rho\alpha$ $\delta\acute{\iota}\kappa\alpha\iota\sigma\nu$.

THIRD SAYING. ll. 21–7.

[λέγει Ἰη(σοῦ)ς·
οὐκ ἀποκνήσει ἄνθ[ρωπος . . . . . .
ρων ἐπερωτῆσαι πα[. . . . .
ρων περὶ τοῦ τόπου τῆ[ς . . . .
25 σετε ὅτι πολλοὶ ἔσονται π[ρῶτοι ἔσχατοι καὶ
οἱ ἔσχατοι πρῶτοι καὶ [. . . . .
σιν.

'Jesus saith, A man shall not hesitate . . . to ask . . .
concerning his place (in the kingdom. Ye shall know) that
many that are first shall be last and the last first and (they
shall have eternal life ?).'

Line 24 may well have continued τ[ῆς βασιλείας followed by
a word meaning 'know'; but in the absence of a clear parallel
we forbear to restore the earlier part of the Saying. Lines 25–6
follow Mark x. 31 (=Matt. xix. 30) 'Many that are first shall
be last, and the last first.' Luke xiii. 30 is rather longer.
'There are last which shall be first and there are first which
shall be last.' σιν in l. 27 is no doubt the termination of a
verb: for 'shall have eternal life' cf. John iii. 16, 36, v. 24, &c.

FOURTH SAYING. ll. 27–31.

λέγει Ἰη(σοῦ)ς· [πᾶν τὸ μὴ ἔμπροσ-
θεν τῆς ὄψεως σου καὶ [τὸ κεκρυμμένον
ἀπὸ σοῦ ἀποκαλυφ⟨θ⟩ήσετ[αί σοι. οὐ γάρ ἐσ-
30 τιν κρυπτὸν ὃ οὐ φανε[ρὸν γενήσεται
καὶ τεθαμμένον ὃ ο[ὐκ ἐγερθήσεται.

'Jesus saith, Everything that is not before thy face and
that which is hidden from thee shall be revealed to thee.
For there is nothing hidden which shall not be made manifest, nor buried which shall not be raised.'

The sense of this Saying is clear, and the supplements are
fairly certain. Lines 29–30 are parallel to Matt. x. 26 'For
there is nothing covered that shall not be revealed, and hid that

shall not be known'; Luke xii. 2 'But there is nothing covered up that shall not be revealed, and hid that shall not be known'; cf. Mark iv. 22 'For there is nothing hid save that it should be manifested, neither was anything made secret but that it should come to light.' In general arrangement the papyrus agrees with the versions of Matthew and Luke perhaps more than with that of Mark; but the language of the first half of the sentence is much closer to St. Mark's (whose expression 'save that it should be manifested' instead of the more pointed 'which shall not be manifested' suggests the hand of an editor), while that of the second half diverges from all three. 'Buried' makes a more forcible contrast to 'hidden' than the corresponding word in the Synoptists, which is merely a synonym for 'hidden.' Instead of 'shall be raised' a more general expression such as 'shall be made known' can be supplied; but this detracts from the picturesqueness of what is in any case a striking variation of a well-known Saying.

FIFTH SAYING. ll. 32–42.

$[\grave{\epsilon}\xi]\epsilon\tau\acute{a}\zeta o\upsilon\sigma\iota\nu \ a\grave{\upsilon}\tau\grave{o}\nu \ o[\grave{\iota} \ \mu a\theta\eta\tau a\grave{\iota} \ a\grave{\upsilon}\tau o\hat{\upsilon} \ \kappa a\grave{\iota}$
$[\lambda\acute{\epsilon}]\gamma o\upsilon\sigma\iota\nu\cdot \ \pi\hat{\omega}\varsigma \ \nu\eta\sigma\tau\epsilon\acute{\upsilon}[\sigma o\mu\epsilon\nu \ \kappa a\grave{\iota} \ \pi\hat{\omega}\varsigma \ \ldots$
$[\ldots\ldots]\mu\epsilon\theta a \ \kappa a\grave{\iota} \ \pi\hat{\omega}\varsigma \ [\ldots\ldots\ldots\ldots\ldots$
35 $[\ldots\ldots \kappa]a\grave{\iota} \ \tau\acute{\iota} \ \pi a\rho a\tau\eta\rho\acute{\eta}\sigma[o\mu\epsilon\nu \ \ldots\ldots\ldots$
$[\ldots\ldots]\nu \ ; \ \lambda\acute{\epsilon}\gamma\epsilon\iota \ \ 'I\eta(\sigma o\hat{\upsilon})\varsigma\cdot \ [\ldots\ldots\ldots\ldots$
$[\ldots\ldots]\epsilon\iota\tau a\iota \ \mu\grave{\eta} \ \pi o\iota\epsilon\hat{\iota}\tau[\epsilon \ \ldots\ldots\ldots$
$[\ldots\ldots]\eta\varsigma \ \grave{a}\lambda\eta\theta\epsilon\acute{\iota}a\varsigma \ \grave{a}\nu[\ldots\ldots\ldots\ldots$
$[\ldots\ldots\ldots\ldots]\nu \ \grave{a}[\pi]o\kappa\epsilon\kappa\rho]\upsilon \ \ldots\ldots\ldots\ldots$
40 $[\ldots\ldots \mu a]\kappa\acute{a}\rho\iota[\acute{o}\varsigma] \ \grave{\epsilon}\sigma\tau\iota\nu \ [\ldots\ldots\ldots\ldots$
$[\ldots\ldots\ldots\ldots]\omega \ \grave{\epsilon}\sigma\tau[\iota \ \ldots\ldots\ldots\ldots$
$[\ldots\ldots\ldots\ldots\ldots]\iota\nu[\ldots\ldots\ldots\ldots\ldots$

'His disciples question him and say, How shall we fast and how shall we (pray ?) . . . and what (commandment) shall we keep . . . Jesus saith, . . . do not . . . of truth . . . blessed is he . . .'

Though this Saying is broken beyond hope of recovery, its general drift may be caught. It clearly differed from the other

Sayings, both in this papyrus and the first series of Logia, in having a preliminary paragraph giving the occasion, which seems to be a question put by the disciples. This question consisted of a number of short sentences, each beginning with 'how' or 'what,' and so far as can be judged, they were concerned with the outward forms of religion, fasting, prayer, and almsgiving. How far, it was probably asked, are existing Jewish ordinances to be kept? The answer of Jesus appears to have been a series of short commandments insisting on the inner side of religion as the pursuit of virtue and truth, and very likely concluding in l. 40 with the promise 'Blessed is he who doeth these things.' If this explanation is on the right lines, there is a general parallelism between this Saying and Matt. xix. 16–22 and Luke xviii. 18–22 (the answer to the question 'What shall I do to inherit eternal life?'). The reference to fasting in l. 33 suggests a connexion with the 2nd Logion ('Except ye fast to the world'), which may well have been an answer to a similar question by the disciples.

(d) GENERAL REMARKS.

We do not propose to enter upon a detailed examination of the numerous and complicated problems involving the Canonical and Apocryphal Gospels and the 'Logia' of 1897, which are reopened by the discovery of the new Sayings. But we may be permitted to indicate the broader issues at stake, and in the light of the wide discussion of the Logia of 1897 to point out some effects of the new elements now introduced into the controversy.

We start therefore with a comparison of the two series of Sayings, which we shall henceforth call 1 (the new Sayings) and 2 (the 'Logia' found in 1897). Both were found on the same site and the papyri are of approximately the same date, which is not later than about the middle of the third century, so that both collections must go back at least to the second century. The outward appearance of the two papyri is indeed different, 2 being a leaf from a handsomely-written book, which may well have been a valuable trade-copy, while 1 is in roll

form and was written on the back of a comparatively trivial
document.   The practice of writing important literary texts on
such material was, however, extremely common, and the form
of 1 lends no support to the hypothesis that the papyrus is a
collection of notes made by the writer himself.   In the uncial
character of the handwriting, the absence of abbreviations and
contractions other than those usually found in early theological MSS., and the careful punctuation, 1 shares the character-
istics of an ordinary literary text such as 2. . Since 2 is the
11th page of a book, it must have formed part of a large collection of Sayings, while 1 comes from the beginning of a
manuscript and provides no direct evidence of the length of
the roll.   But the document on the other side is not a letter
or contract which would be likely to be short, but an official
land-survey list, and these tend to be of very great length ; so
far therefore as can be judged from externals, 1 like 2 probably belongs to an extensive collection of Sayings which may
well have numbered several hundreds.

Turning next to the contents of the two papyri, no one can
fail to be struck with their formal resemblance.   Postponing
for the moment the introduction of 1 (ll. 1–5), which, since it
necessarily presupposes the existence of the Sayings introduced
and may have been added later, stands on a different footing
from the Sayings and requires separate treatment, the five
Sayings partly recorded in 1 begin like those in 2 with the
plain formula ' Jesus saith ' ; and both fragments contain Sayings which to a greater or less degree have parallel passages
in the Synoptic Gospels side by side with Sayings which are
new.   In 2 the style was simple and direct, and the setting,
with the constant balancing of the words and sentences and
the absence of connecting particles, highly archaic ; the same
features, though obscured unfortunately by the incompleteness
of the papyrus, are also distinctly traceable in 1.   There is,
however, one difference in the two papyri in point of form.
To the 5th Saying in 1 (ll. 36 sqq.) is prefixed (ll. 32–6) a brief
account of the question to which it was the answer ; but this
is the exception, not the rule, and the fact that the Sayings in 2
agree with the first four Sayings in 1 in omitting the context

rather than with the 5th obviously produces no serious conflict between the two documents.

We proceed to a closer examination of the two series. In 2 the 7th Logion ('A city built on a hill') is connected with St. Matthew's Gospel alone; the 6th ('A prophet is not accept-able') has a marked point of contact with St. Luke in the use of the word 'acceptable,' and the 1st also agrees with St. Luke. The 5th ('Wherever there are') starts with a parallel to St. Matthew, but extends into a region far beyond. Nowhere in 2 can the influence of St. Mark be traced, nor was there any direct parallel with St. John's Gospel; but the new matter, both in thought and expression, tended to have a mystical and Johan-nine character. In 1 we have one Saying (the 2nd) of which the central idea is parallel to a passage found in St. Luke alone, but of which the developments are new; the conclusion of the 3rd Saying connects with St. Matthew and St. Mark rather than with St. Luke, while the 4th is a different version of a Saying found in all three Synoptists, and is on the whole nearer to St. Mark than to the other two Evangelists. The 1st Saying and, so far as we can judge, the 5th have little, if any, point of contact with the Canonical Gospels. As in 2, so in 1 the new elements tend to have a Johannine colouring, especially in the 2nd Saying; and though the Sayings in 1 contain nothing so markedly Johannine in style as e. g. 'I stood in the midst of the world . . .' in 2, the introduction contains a clear parallel to John viii. 52. This at first sight may perhaps seem to im-ply a knowledge of St. John's Gospel on the part of the author of the introduction, but it must be remembered (1) that St. John may well not have been the sole authority for the attribution of that Saying to our Lord, and if so, that the author of the in-troduction may have obtained it from another source, (2) that a knowledge of St. John's Gospel on the part of the author of the introduction .does not necessarily imply a corresponding debt to that Gospel in the following Sayings, which, as we have said, stand on a somewhat different footing from the introduc-tion.

In our original edition of 2 we maintained (*a*) that the Say-ings had no traceable thread of connexion with each other beyond the fact of their being ascribed to the same speaker, (*b*) that none of them implied a post-resurrectional point of view, (*c*) that they were not in themselves heretical, and that though the asceticism of Log. 2 and the mystic character of Log. 5 were obviously capable of development in Encratite and Gnostic directions, the Sayings as a whole were much nearer in style to the New Testament than to the apocryphal literature of the middle and end of the second century. If these positions have been vigorously assailed, they have also been stoutly defended, and about the second and third no general agreement has been reached ; with regard to the first the balance of opinion has been in favour of our view, and the various attempts to trace a connexion of ideas running through the Sayings have met with little acceptance. What answer is to be returned to the corresponding problems in **1** ?

We will take the third question first. Is there anything in **1** to show that the Sayings originated in or circulated among a particular sect ?. We should answer this in the negative. There is nothing heretical in the introduction, the 1st, 3rd, and 4th Sayings, or, so far as can be judged, the 5th. The Ascetic leanings which have been ascribed to the 2nd Logion are conspicuously absent in **1** ; the remains of the 5th Saying in fact rather suggest an anti-Jewish point of view, from which however the 2nd Logion itself was not widely distant, if, as we strongly hold, 'fast' and 'sabbatize' are to be taken metaphorically. The absence of any Jewish-Christian element in **1** is the more remarkable seeing that the 1st Saying also occurs in the Gospel according to the Hebrews. The only Saying that is at all suspicious is the 2nd, which like Log. 5 is sure to be called in some quarters 'Gnostic.' That the profoundly mystical but, as it seems to us, obviously genuine Saying of our Lord recorded in Luke xvii. 21 ' The kingdom of God is within you ' should have given rise to much speculation was to be expected, and from Hippolytus *Refut.* v. 7 it is known that this Saying occupied an important place in the doctrines of the Naassenes, one of the most pronounced Gnostic sects of the second or early third century. That there is a connexion between the Sayings and the Naassenes through the Gospel of Thomas is quite possible and this point will be discussed later; but to import Naassene tenets into the 2nd Saying in 1 is not only gratuitous but a ὕστερον πρότερον. Moreover, though the other ideas in the Saying connected with the parallel from St. Luke, the development of the kingdom of Heaven through brute creation up to man (if that be the meaning of ll. 9–16), and the Christian turn given to the proverbial 'Know thyself' (ll. 16–21), may point to a later stage of thought than that found in the Canonical Gospels, the 2nd Saying as a whole, if 'Gnostic,' presents a very primitive kind of Gnosticism, and is widely separated from the fully-developed theosophy of e. g. the *Pistis Sophia*.   In any case the 'Gnosticism' of 1 is on much the same level as that of 2.

Do any of the Sayings (apart from the introduction) imply a post-resurrectional point of view? This too we should answer in the negative.   There is not only nothing in them to indicate that they were spoken after the resurrection, but substantial evidence for the opposite view.   The familiar Sayings in the Canonical Gospels which are parallel to those found in 1 are there assigned to our Lord's lifetime, including even John viii. 52.   The Gospel according to the Hebrews with which the 1st Saying is connected covered the same ground as the Synoptists, and there is no reason to suppose that this Saying occurred there as a post-resurrectional utterance.   But the best argument is provided by the 5th Saying, especially its context, which is fortunately given.   The questions there addressed to Jesus clearly belong to a class of problems which are known to have been raised by our Lord's disciples and others in his lifetime, and, if ἐξετάζουσιν is in any case a somewhat stronger term than would be expected, seeing that the disciples seem to be the subject (though cf. John xxi. 12), it is most unlikely that this word would have been used with reference to the risen Christ.   In fact none of the five Sayings in 1 suggests a post-resurrectional point of view so much as the 3rd Logion ('I stood in the midst of the world'); cf. p. 26.

Can a definite principle or train of ideas be traced through the Sayings? The first four are certainly linked together by the connecting idea of the kingdom of Heaven, which is the subject to a greater or less degree of all of them.   But between

the 4th and the 5th Sayings the chain is certainly much weaker
and threatens to snap altogether. It is very difficult to believe
that if **1** was part of a large collection of similar Sayings a connexion of thought could have been maintained throughout, and
the Sayings in the later columns of **1** may well have been as
disconnected as those in **2**. Even in the five which are partly
preserved in **1** there is a constant change in the persons addressed, the 1st and 3rd being couched in the third singular,
the 2nd and almost certainly the 5th in the second plural, and
the 4th in the second singular. Moreover the real link is, we
think, supplied by the introduction, the consideration of which
can no longer be delayed. Only before proceeding further we
would state our conviction that in all essential points, the date
of the papyrus, the form of the Sayings, their relation to the
Canonical Gospels, and the general character of the new elements in them, to say nothing of the parallelism of thought
between the 1st and 3rd Sayings and the 5th Logion, the resemblances between **1** and **2** so far outweigh the differences
that for practical purposes they may be treated as parts of the
same collection.

' *These are the . . . words which Jesus the living* (*Lord*) *spake
to . . . and Thomas, and he said unto* (*them*) " *Every one that
hearkens to these words shall never taste of death.*" ' Such is
the remarkable opening prefixed to the collection of Sayings in
1 by its unknown editor. The first point to be noticed is that
the name given to the collection is, as was acutely divined by
Dr. Lock (*Two Lectures on the Sayings of Jesus*, p. 16), *Logoi*,
not *Logia*, and all questions concerning the meaning of the
latter term may therefore be left out of account in dealing with
the present series of Sayings. The converse of this, however,
in our opinion by no means holds good, and as we have pointed
out (pp. 12–3), the analogy of the present document has a considerable bearing upon the problems concerning an early collection of ' Logia.' Secondly, the collection is represented as
being spoken either to St. Thomas alone or to St. Thomas and
another disciple or, less probably, other disciples. Does the
compiler mean that the Sayings were the subject of a special revelation to St. Thomas and perhaps another disciple, from which

the rest were excluded? The case in favour of an affirmative answer to this query would be greatly strengthened if the introduction provided any indication that the editor assigned his collection of Sayings to the period after the Resurrection. But no such evidence is forthcoming. In the Canonical Gospels St. Thomas is indeed made prominent only in connexion with that period (John xx. 24 sqq.), but this circumstance, which is probably the strongest argument in favour of a post-resurrectional point of view, is discounted by the fact that the Gospel of Thomas, so far as can be judged, was not of the nature of a post-resurrectional Gospel but rather a Gospel of the childhood (cf. p. 32), and, secondly, seems to be outweighed by the indications in the Sayings themselves that some of them at any rate were assigned to Jesus' lifetime. We are not therefore disposed to consider that the introduction to the Sayings, any more than the Sayings by themselves, implies a post-resurrectional point of view on the part of the compiler. What we think he did mean to imply was that the ultimate authority for the record of these Sayings was in his opinion St. Thomas or St. Thomas and another disciple. This hypothesis provides a satisfactory, in fact we think the only satisfactory, explanation of the frequent changes of persons and abrupt transitions of subject which characterize the Sayings as a whole.

What value, if any, is to be attached to this far-reaching claim — that the collection of Sayings derives its authority, not from the traditional sources of any of the four Canonical Gospels, but from St. Thomas and perhaps another disciple? The custom of invoking the authority of a great and familiar name for an anonymous and later work is so common in early Christian, as in other, writings, that the mere statement of the editor carries no weight by itself, and is not worth considering unless the internal evidence of the Sayings themselves can be shown to point in the same direction, or at any rate to be not inconsistent with his claim. We pass, therefore, to the problem of the general nature and origin of the Sayings in 1 and 2, and as a convenient method of inquiry start from an examination of some of the various theories already put forward in explanation of 2. A useful bibliography and *résumé* of the controversy will be found in Professors Lock and Sanday's *Two Lectures on the Sayings of Jesus*.

In our original edition of 2 we proposed A. D. 140 as the latest date to which the composition of the Sayings could be referred. This *terminus ad quem* has generally been accepted, by even Dr. Sanday, who is amongst the most conservative of our critics; and we should propose A. D. 140 for the *terminus ad quem* in reference to 1 with greater confidence than we felt about 2 in 1897.

The chief dividing line in the controversy lies between those who agreed with our suggestion that 2 belonged to a collection of Sayings as such, and those who considered 2 to be a series of extracts from one or more of the numerous extra-canonical gospels which are known to have circulated in Egypt in the second century. Does 1 help to decide the question in either direction? One argument which has been widely used in support of the view that 2 was really a series of extracts, viz. that the Sayings had no contexts, is somewhat damaged by the appearance of a Saying which has a context. But the formal presence or absence of contexts in a series of Sayings can be employed with equal plausibility to prove or disprove the view that the series consisted of extracts, and would therefore seem a very unsound argument to introduce into the discussion. The matter of the context of the 5th Saying, however, has perhaps a more important bearing than the form upon the question of extracts. The phrase ' Jesus saith ' there follows two historic presents, ' question ' and ' say,' and is therefore presumably itself a historic present; and if ' Jesus saith ' is a historic present in one case, it should be so throughout 1 and 2. Is it then probable that the formula ' Jesus saith ' has been taken over without alteration by the editor from his source, which was therefore presumably a Gospel narrative? To this we should answer by a decided negative. It is not likely that the present tense ' saith ' would have been uniformly employed in a narrative, and yet 1 provides at least three more instances of the phrase ' Jesus saith ' (ll. 9, 27, and 36). It is, we think, much more probable that the formula is due to the editor of the collection than to his sources, whatever they were. And

though there is now no longer any particular reason for inter-
preting the tense of 'saith' as more than a historic present, a
secondary meaning is not excluded, and may be present in
l. 36 just as much as in the other instances where there is no
context. We should be inclined to paraphrase 'Jesus saith'
as 'This is one of those Sayings of Jesus to which I referred
in the introduction,' and to explain the uniform repetition of
it as marking off the several Sayings from each other, and giving greater impressiveness to the whole. The fact that the
editor used the aorist and not the historic present in his introduction suggests that by his employment of the present tense
'saith' throughout the Sayings he intended to produce a
slightly different effect from that which would have been caused
by 'said.' But this new light shed upon the formula 'Jesus
saith' does not bring with it any new reason for regarding the
Sayings as extracts from a narrative Gospel.

A much more important factor in deciding whether the Sayings are extracts or not is the introduction, which though it
may be a later addition, and though the reference to St. Thomas
may be merely a bold invention of the editor, is there, and its
presence has to be accounted for. So far from stating that
the Sayings are extracts from any work, the editor asserts that
they are a collection of Sayings, a circumstance which seems to
provide an adequate explanation not only of the disconnected
character of the Sayings in part of the collection, but of the
repetition of the formula 'Jesus saith' before each one. It is
now clear that l was meant by the editor to be regarded as an
independent literary work, complete in itself ; and though it is
not necessary to accept it as such, those who wish to maintain
that the collection is something quite different from what it
purports to be must be prepared to explain how the introduction comes to be there. Hence we think that no theory of the
origin of the Sayings as a whole is to be considered satisfactory
unless it at the same time provides a reasonable explanation of
the fact that some one not later than the middle of the second
century published the Sayings as specially connected with St.
Thomas (and perhaps another disciple), and that the collection
attained sufficient importance for it to be read, and presumably

accepted as genuine, in the chief towns of Upper Egypt in the century following.

Among the different explanations of 2 which have been put forward the most generally accepted is probably that maintained, with all his usual brilliant powers of analysis, by Professor Harnack, that 2 consisted of extracts from the Gospel according to the Egyptians, an early Gospel covering apparently the same ground as the Synoptists and circulating principally in Egypt, where it was probably composed. The question was, however, complicated by the extremely divergent views held concerning the importance and heretical character of that Gospel, to which only one passage of any length can be assigned with certainty (cf. p. 43, where a translation of it is given). There is little if any relation between that extract and anything in 2; and disagreeing as we do with Harnack's view of the Gospel according to the Egyptians, we have never been able to regard his explanation of 2 as satisfactory. The evidence of 1 provides fresh objections to the theory. There is no direct point of contact between 1 and the Gospel according to the Egyptians, and where one of the uncanonical Sayings happens to be known it occurs not in this Gospel but in that according to the Hebrews. There is, indeed, more to be said for regarding 1 as extracts from the latter Gospel, as has been suggested in the case of 2 by more than one critic, than from the Gospel according to the Egyptians. In their divergence from the Canonical Gospels, the striking character of much of the new matter, the Hebraic parallelisms of expression, the Sayings are quite in keeping with the style of the most venerable and important of all the uncanonical Gospels, which is known to have been written originally in Hebrew, and which is now generally regarded as independent of the four Canonical Gospels and but little later than the Synoptists in date. To these points of connexion has now to be added the far more solid piece of evidence afforded by the 1st Saying in 1. There remain indeed the objections (cf. *Sayings of our Lord*, p. 17) that the Gospel according to the Hebrews would be expected to show greater resemblance to St. Matthew than we find in 2 and 1, which is even further away from St. Matthew's Gospel

than 2, and secondly that the Johannine colouring traceable in
the new Sayings is foreign to the extant fragments of the Gospel according to the Hebrews, which seems to have been quite
parallel to the Synoptists.   But it is quite possible that the
Gospel according to the Hebrews had a mystical side which is
revealed to us occasionally (as e. g. in the curious passage in
which Jesus speaks of his ' mother, the Holy Ghost,' and in
the Saying found also in 1), but which owing to the paucity of
references has hitherto been underestimated.   A far graver
and in fact almost fatal objection, however, to regarding the
Sayings as extracts culled from either the Gospel according
to the Hebrews or the Gospel according to the Egyptians is
the irreconcilability of such a view with the introduction of 1.
It is very difficult to believe that an editor would have had the
boldness to issue extracts from such widely known works as
an independent collection of Sayings claiming the authority of
Thomas and perhaps another disciple.   Even if we supply ' to
Matthew' in 1. 2 before 'and Thomas' and suppose that the
mention of Thomas is of quite secondary importance, it is very
hard to supply a reasonable motive for issuing a series of
extracts from the Gospel according to the Hebrews with such
a preface as we find in 1, and to account for the popularity of
these supposed extracts in the century following their publication.   We are therefore on the whole opposed to the view,
attractive though it undoubtedly is, that the Sayings are all
directly derived from the Gospel according to the Hebrews.
But that there is a connexion between them is certain, and it
is significant that the *Stromateis* of Clement of Alexandria, in
which work Dr. Mayor (*ap.* Rendel Harris, *Contemp. Rev.* 1897,
pp. 344–5) has with much probability detected references to
the 2nd Logion, are also the source of the quotation from the
Gospel according to the Hebrews which is closely parallel to
the 1st Saying.   It is not at all unlikely that the 2nd Logion
(' Except ye fast ') also presented a strong similarity to a passage in the same Gospel.

Both views which we have discussed so far have, whether
satisfactory or not on other grounds, been confronted by the
initial difficulty of the introduction.   Let us now consider the

Gospel ascribed to the disciple whose name occurs in l. 3.   It
is obvious that the introduction would suit a series of extracts
from the Gospel of Thomas much better than one from the
Gospel according to the Hebrews.   The Gospel of Thomas is
known to have existed in more than one form, namely as an
account of Jesus' childhood which is extant in several late re-
censions of varying length, and as an earlier Gospel condemned
by Hippolytus in the following passage (*Refut.* v. 7)   'But
they (sc. the Naassenes) assert that not only is there in favour
of their doctrine testimony to be drawn from the mysteries of
the Assyrians, but also from those of the Phrygians concerning the happy nature, concealed and yet at the same time dis-
closed, of things that have been and are coming into existence
and moreover will be, (a happy nature) which, (the Naassene)
says, is the kingdom of heaven to be sought for within a man.
And concerning this (nature) they hand down an explicit
passage occurring in the Gospel inscribed " according to
Thomas," expressing themselves thus : " He who seeks me
will find me in children from seven years old ; for there concealed I shall in the fourteenth age (or aeon) be made manifest." '   Here we have two remarkable points of contact
with 1, the mention of Thomas coupled with the ' kingdom of
heaven within a man ' (cf. the 2nd Saying).   The parallels between 2 and one of the later forms of the Thomas Gospel have
been worked out with great ingenuity and elaboration by Dr.
Taylor on pp. 90–8 of *The Oxyrhynchus Logia and the Apocryphal Gospels.*   There is much to be said for his view that the
extant Gospel of Thomas contains some traces of 2, and the
probability would be increased if 2, which Dr. Taylor was
inclined to regard as extracts from the Gospel according to the
Egyptians, be supposed to be derived from the earlier Gospel
of Thomas. 1 does not seem to contain any clear points of
connexion with the later Gospel of Thomas, but this is com-
pensated for by the remarkable parallel from Hippolytus quoted
above.   It is moreover noteworthy, as Mr. Badham remarks,
that the Acts of Thomas, which may well have been partly
built upon the Gospel, exhibit a knowledge of that Saying
which occurs both in the Gospel according to the Hebrews and

in 1 (cf. p. 15), and that, as Professor Lake informs us, an Athos MS. (*Studia Biblica*, v. 2, p. 173) asserts that the story of Christ and the woman taken in adultery (which has found its way from the Gospel according to the Hebrews into St. John's Gospel) occurred in the Gospel of Thomas. But there are serious objections to regarding 1 and 2 as extracts from that Gospel. In the first place though it is possible that Thomas is the only disciple mentioned in the introduction, it is equally possible that he stood second, and in that case the Gospel from which the Sayings may have been extracted is more likely to have been one which went under the name of the person who stood first; though indeed, if there were two disciples mentioned in the introduction, it is not very satisfactory to derive the Sayings from any Gospel which went under the name of only one. A much greater difficulty arises from the divergence of the Sayings from what little is known about the earlier Gospel of Thomas. The saying quoted by Hippolytus is widely removed in character from those in 1 and 2; and although the Gospel of Thomas has been placed before A. D. 180, yet from the quotation in Hippolytus, coupled with the form of the Gospel in later times and the scanty evidence from other sources, it has been generally considered to have been mainly at any rate a gospel of the childhood and of an advanced Gnostic character. If the Sayings are to be derived from it, the current view of the Gospel of Thomas must be entirely changed; and it is very doubtful whether this can be done except by postulating the existence of an original Thomas Gospel behind that condemned by Hippolytus. This would lead us into a region of pure conjecture upon which we are unwilling to enter, at any rate until other less hazardous roads to a solution are closed. That there is a connexion between the earlier Gospel of Thomas and the Sayings is extremely likely, but this can be better explained by supposing that the Sayings influenced the Gospel than by the hypothesis that the Gospel is the source of the Sayings.

Our conclusion, therefore, is that neither the Gospel according to the Egyptians, nor that according to the Hebrews, nor that according to Thomas, still less any of the other known

uncanonical Gospels, is a suitable source for the Sayings as a
whole. There is more to be said for explaining them as a series
of extracts from several of these Gospels, as was suggested
with regard to 2 by Dr. James, though this view evades rather
than solves the problem. The occurrence of a Saying which
is known to have been also found in the Gospel according to
the Hebrews, side by side with other Sayings which it is difficult
to ascribe to the same source, rather favours the theory of an
eclectic series derived from different Gospels. But the introduction connecting the Sayings with particular disciples is not
very suitable for such a collection which *ex hypothesi* is of an
altogether miscellaneous character; and in our opinion the
Sayings are much more likely to be a source utilized in one or
more of the uncanonical Gospels, than vice versa. The probability of the general explanation of 2 which we suggested in
1897 and which has been supported by many critics, amongst
others Drs. Swete, Rendel Harris, Sanday, Lock, and Heinrici,
that it was part of a collection of Sayings as such, is largely
increased by the discovery of 1, with its introduction to the
whole collection stating that it was a collection of *Logoi*, which
was obviously intended to stand as an independent literary
work. In fact we doubt if theories of extracts are any longer
justifiable; and in any case such explanations will henceforth
be placed at the initial disadvantage of starting with an assump-
tion which is distinctly contradicted by the introduction of 1.
It is of course possible to explain away this introduction, but
unless very strong reasons can be adduced for doing so, the
simpler and far safer course is to accept the editor's statement
that 1, to which, as we have said, 2 is closely allied, is a collection of Sayings of Jesus.

The opinions of those critics who agreed with our general
explanation of 2 as against the various theories of extracts may
be divided into two classes: (1) those who regarded 2 as a
collection of Sayings independent of the Gospels and belonging
to the first century, and who therefore were disposed to admit
to a greater or less extent and with much varying degrees of
confidence the presence of genuine elements in the new matter
(Drs. Swete, Rendel Harris, Lock, and Heinrici); (2) those

who, like Dr. Sanday, regarded the new Sayings in 2 as the product of the early second century, not directly dependent on the Canonical Gospels, but having 'their origin under conditions of thought which these Gospels had created' (Sanday, *op. cit.* p. 41), a view which necessarily carries with it the rejection of the new matter. It remains to ask how far 1 helps to decide the points at issue in favour of either side.

With regard to the relation of 1 to the Canonical Gospels, the proportion of new and old matter is about the same as in 2, and the parallels to the Canonical Gospels in 1 exhibit the same freedom of treatment, which can be explained either as implying independence of the Canonical Gospels, or as the liberties taken by an early redactor. The introduction in 1 contains a clearer parallel to St. John's Gospel than anything to be found in 2; but even if it be conceded that the introduction implied a knowledge of St. John's Gospel, and was therefore probably composed in the second century, the Sayings themselves can (and, as we shall show, do) contain at any rate some elements which are not derived from the Canonical Gospels, and go back to the first century. So far as the evidence of 1 goes, there is nothing to cause any one to renounce opinions which he may have formed concerning the relation of 2 to the Canonical Gospels. No one who feels certain on this point with regard to the one, is likely to be convinced of the incorrectness of his view by the other.

Secondly, with regard to the new matter in 1, the uncertainties attaching to the restoration and meaning of most of the 2nd, the earlier part of the 3rd, and all the 5th Saying, unfortunately prevent them from being of much use for purposes of critical analysis. Only with regard to the 1st Saying ('Let not him that seeketh cease') are we on quite sure ground. Concerning this striking sentence, as we have said, the most diverse opinions have been held; but the balance of recent criticism is in favour of accepting it as genuine, though on account of the absence of widely attested authority for it, it is not placed in the highest class of genuine Sayings which includes 'It is more blessed to give than to receive.' The occurrence of the Saying in 1 is a new argument for its authority. But whatever view be taken

of its authenticity, and however the connexion between 1 and
the Gospel according to the Hebrews is to be explained, the 1st
Saying in 1 establishes one important fact.   Dr. Sanday may
be right in regarding A. D. 100 as the *terminus a quo* for the
composition of 2, and the same *terminus a quo* can of course be
assigned to 1 in the sense that the Sayings were not put together and the introduction not written before that date.   But,
if we may accept the agreement of the leading theologians that
the Gospel of the Hebrews was written in the first century, 'it
is impossible any longer to deny that 1 and therefore, as we
maintain, 2, contain some non-canonical elements which directly
or indirectly go back to the first century ; and the existence of
first century elements in one case certainly increases the probability of their presence in others.   In this respect, therefore,
1 provides a remarkable confirmation of the views of those
critics who were prepared to allow a first century date for the
' Logia' of 1897, and accordingly to treat them as reflecting a
substantially authentic tradition.

Are we then, adapting to 1 Dr. Sanday's view of 2 with the
fewest possible modifications, to regard the whole collection as
a free compilation in the early part of the second century, by
an Alexandrian Jewish-Christian, of Sayings ultimately derived
from the Canonical Gospels, and very likely the Gospels according to the Hebrews and Thomas, and perhaps others as well ;
and shall we dismiss the new elements, except the 1st Saying
in 1, as the spurious accretions of an age of philosophic speculation, and surroundings of dubious orthodoxy ?   Even so the
two papyri are of great interest as revealing a hitherto unknown
development of primitive belief upon the nature of Christ's
teaching, and supplying new and valuable evidence for deter-
mining the relationship of the uncanonical Gospels to the main
current of orthodox Christianity.   Or are we rather to consider
1 and 2 to be fragments of an early collection of our Lord's
Sayings in a form which has been influenced to some extent
by the thought and literature of the apostolic and post-apostolic
age, and which may well itself have influenced the Gospel
of Thomas and perhaps others of the heretical Gospels, but
which is ultimately connected in a large measure with a first-

hand source other than that of any of the Canonical Gospels?
Some such view has been maintained by scholars of eminence,
e. g. Heinrici and Rendel Harris, with regard to 2; and if
the claim made by the editor of the collection in his introduction, that his source was St. Thomas and perhaps another
disciple, amounts to but little more, the internal evidence of 1
provides no obvious reason why we should concede him much
less ; while the occurrence of one uncanonical Saying, which
is already known to be of extreme antiquity and has been
accepted as substantially genuine by several critics, lends considerable support to the others which rest on the evidence of 1
and 2 alone.

That is as far as we are prepared to go ; for a really weighty
and perfectly unbiassed estimate of the ultimate value of any
new discovery, resort must be made to some other quarter than
the discoverers. We conclude by pointing out that, if the view
with regard to the Sayings which we have just indicated is on
the right lines, the analogy of this collection has an obvious
bearing on the question of the sources of the Synoptic Gospels,
and that the mystical and speculative element in the early
records of Christ's Sayings which found its highest and most
widely accepted expression in St. John's Gospel, may well have
been much more general and less peculiarly Johannine than
has hitherto been taken for granted.

II. THE 'LOGIA' DISCOVERED IN 1897

(THE OXYRHYNCHUS PAPYRI, Part I, 1.)

Logion 1.

. . . καὶ τότε διαβλέψεις ἐκβαλεῖν τὸ κάρφος τὸ ἐν τῷ ὀφθαλμῷ τοῦ ἀδελφοῦ σου.

'. . . and then shalt thou see clearly to cast out the mote that is in thy brother's eye.'

Logion 2.

Λέγει Ἰησοῦς, ἐὰν μὴ νηστεύσητε τὸν κόσμον οὐ μὴ εὕρητε τὴν βασιλείαν τοῦ θεοῦ· καὶ ἐὰν μὴ σαββατίσητε τὸ σάββατον οὐκ ὄψεσθε τὸν πατέρα.

'Jesus saith, Except ye fast to the world, ye shall in no wise find the kingdom of God ; and except ye make the sabbath a real sabbath, ye shall not see the Father.'

Logion 3.

Λέγει Ἰησοῦς, ἔ[σ]την ἐν μέσῳ τοῦ κόσμου καὶ ἐν σαρκὶ ὤφθην αὐτοῖς, καὶ εὗρον πάντας μεθύοντας καὶ οὐδένα εὗρον διψῶντα ἐν αὐτοῖς, καὶ πονεῖ ἡ ψυχή μου ἐπὶ τοῖς υἱοῖς τῶν ἀνθρώπων, ὅτι τυφλοί εἰσιν τῇ καρδίᾳ αὐτῶ[ν] καὶ οὐ βλέ[πουσιν . . .

'Jesus saith, I stood in the midst of the world and in the flesh was I seen of them, and I found all men drunken, and none found I athirst among them, and my soul grieveth over the sons of men, because they are blind in their heart and see not . . .'

Logion 4.

. . . τ]ὴν πτωχείαν.

'. . . poverty.'

Logion 5.

[Λέγ]ει ['Ιησοῦς, ὅη]ου ἐὰν ὦσιν [β̄ οὐκ] ε[ἰσι]ν
ἄθεοι, καὶ [ὅ]που ε[ἷς] ἐστιν μόνος, [λέ]γω, ἐγώ εἰμι
μετ' αὐτ[οῦ·] ἔγει[ρ]ον τὸν λίθον κἀκεῖ εὑρήσεις με,
σχίσον τὸ ξύλον κἀγὼ ἐκεῖ εἰμι.

'Jesus saith, Wherever there are (two), they are not
without God, and wherever there is one alone, I say, I am
with him.   Raise the stone, and there thou shalt find me ;
cleave the wood, and there am I.'

Logion 6.

Λέγει 'Ιησοῦς, οὐκ ἔστιν δεκτὸς προφήτης ἐν τῇ πατρίδι
αὐτ[ο]ῦ, οὐδὲ ἰατρὸς ποιεῖ θεραπείας εἰς τοὺς γινώσκοντας
αὐτόν.

'Jesus saith, A prophet is not acceptable in his own
country, neither doth a physician work cures upon them
that know him.'

Logion 7.

Λέγει 'Ιησοῦς, πόλις ᾠκοδομημένη ἐπ' ἄκρον [ὄ]ρους
ὑψηλοῦ καὶ ἐστηριγμένη οὔτε πε[σ]εῖν δύναται οὔτε
κρυ[β]ῆναι.

'Jesus saith, A city built upon the top of a high hill and
stablished, can neither fall nor be hid.'

Logion 8.

Λέγει 'Ιησοῦς, ἀκούεις [ε]ἰς τὸ ἐν ὠτίον σου, τὸ [δὲ
ἕτερον συνέκλεισας].

'Jesus saith, Thou hearest with one ear, (but the other
thou hast closed).'

III. FRAGMENT OF A LOST GOSPEL

(a) INTRODUCTION.

EIGHT fragments of a papyrus in roll form containing a lost Gospel, the largest (*b*) measuring 8.2 × 8.3 *cm.* and comprising parts of the middles of two narrow columns. None of the other fragments actually joins (*b*), but it is practically certain that the relation to it of Frs. (*a*) and (*c*), which come from the tops of columns, is as indicated in the text. Frs. (*d*) and (*e*), both of which have a margin below the writing, probably belong to the bottom of the same two columns which are partly preserved in (*b*); but how much is lost in the interval is uncertain. Since the upper portion of Col. i admits of a sure restoration of the majority of the lacunae, the first 23 lines are nearly complete; but the remains of the second column are for the most part too slight for the sense to be recovered. The handwriting is a small uncial of the common sloping oval type, which in most cases belongs to the third century. The papyrus is a well-written specimen, suggesting the earlier rather than the later period during which this hand was in vogue, and though we should not assign it to the second century, it is not likely to have been written later than A. D. 250. Lines 1–16 give the conclusion of a discourse of Jesus which is parallel to several sentences in the Sermon on the Mount. Then follows (ll. 17–23) an account of a question put to Him by the disciples and of the answer. This, the most important part of the papyrus, is new, but bears an interesting resemblance to a known quotation from the Gospel according to the Egyptians; cf. note *ad loc.* A passage in Col. ii seems to be parallel to Luke xi. 52. On the general questions concerning the nature and origin of the Gospel to which the fragment belonged see pp. 45–7.

(b) TEXT.

Col. i.

(a) [. . .]ΠΟ ΠΡΩΙ Є[. . . . .
   [. . . .]Є ΑΦ ЄСΠ[. . . . .
   [. . . .]ΡΩΙ ΜΗΤЄ [. . . .
   [. . . . . .]ΜΩΝ ΤΙ ΦΑ[
5 [. . . . .] ΤΗ СΤ[.
   [. . . . . . .] ΤΙ ЄΝΔΥ[.

(b) [. .]ϹΘЄ [. . .]ΛΩ ΚΡЄΙ[.
   [. . .]ЄϹ . [. . .] ΤΩΝ [. .
   ΝΩΝ ΑΤΙ[. . .]ΥΞΑ[.
10 ΝЄΙ ΟΥΔЄ Ν[. .]ЄΙ . [.
   ЄΝ ЄΧΟΝΤ[. . .]ΝΑ[.
   ΜΑ ΤΙ ЄΝ[. . . .] ΚΑΙ
   ΥΜЄΙϹ ΤΙϹ ΑΝ ΠΡΟϹΘΗ
   ЄΠΙ ΤΗΝ ЄΙΛΙΚΙΑΝ
15 ΥΜΩΝ ΑΥΤΟ[. .]ΩϹЄΙ
   ΥΜЄΙΝ ΤΟ ЄΝΔΥΜΑ Υ
   ΜΩΝ ΛЄΓΟΥϹΙΝ ΑΥ
   ΤΩ ΟΙ ΜΑΘΗΤΑΙ ΑΥΤΟΥ
   ΠΟΤЄ ΗΜЄΙΝ ЄΜΦΑ
20 ΝΗϹ ЄϹЄΙ ΚΑΙ ΠΟΤЄ
   ϹЄ ΟΨΟΜЄΘΑ ΛЄΓЄΙ
   ΟΤΑΝ ЄΚΔΥϹΗϹΘЄ ΚΑΙ
   ΜΗ ΑΙϹΧΥΝΘΗΤЄ
   . . . .

(d) . . . .
     ]ΤΙΝ
25]ΩΤΙΝ
   ]ΟϹΜΩ
     ]Η
   ]ϹΤΙΝ

Col. ii.

(c) Θ[
30 ΛЄ[
   Ο[
   ΤΑ[
   ΓΥ[
   ·ΚΑ[
35 Ν . [
   ΚΑ[
   ΗΜ[
   ϹΙ[
   [
40 [

(b) ЄΛ[
   ΤΗϹ [
   ΚΡΥΨ[
   ЄΙϹΗΛ[
45 ЄΙϹЄΡ[
   ΚΑΝ[
   ΔЄ ΓЄΙ[
   ΜΟΙΩ[
   ΚЄΡΑΙ[
50 ΡΑ[
   . . . .

(e) . . .
   ΚΟ[

(f) . . .   (g) . . .   (h) . . .
   ]ΚΑ[   ]Κ . [   ]Є[
   . . .   ]ΑΙ[. . .
             . . .

[. . ἀ]πὸ πρωὶ ε[ως ὀψὲ
[μήτ]ε ἀφ᾽ ἑσπ[έρας
[ἕως π]ρωὶ μήτε [τῇ
[τροφῇ ὑ]μῶν τί φά-
5 [γητε μήτε] τῇ στ[ο-
[λῇ ὑμῶν] τί ἐνδύ-
[ση]σθε. [πολ]λῷ κρεί[σ-
[σον]ές [ἐστε] τῶν [κρί-
νων ἅτι[να a]ὐξά-
10 νει οὐδὲ ν[ήθ]ει . [.
ἓν ἔχοντ[ες ἔ]νδ[υ-
μα τί ἐν[. . . .] καὶ
ὑμεῖς ; τίς ἂν προσθ⟨εί⟩η
ἐπὶ τὴν ἡλικίαν
15 ὑμῶν ; αὐτὸ[ς δ]ώσει
ὑμῖν τὸ ἔνδυμα ὑ-
μῶν. λέγουσιν αὐ-
τῷ οἱ μαθηταὶ αὐτοῦ·
πότε ἡμῖν ἐμφα-
20 νὴς ἔσει καὶ πότε
σε ὀψόμεθα ; λέγει·
ὅταν ἐκδύσησθε καὶ
μὴ αἰσχυνθῆτε,

· · · · ·

41 ἔλ[εγε· τὴν κλεῖδα
τῆς [γνώσεως ἐ-
κρύψ[ατε· αὐτοὶ οὐκ
εἰσήλ[θατε, καὶ τοῖς
45 εἰσερ[χομένοις οὐ-
κ ἀν[εῴξατε . . . .

· · · · ·

(c) TRANSLATION AND NOTES.

1–23. ' (Take no thought) from morning until even nor
from evening until morning, either for your food what ye
shall eat or for your raiment what ye shall put on. Ye are
far better than the lilies which grow but spin not. Having
one garment, what do ye (lack?) . . . Who could add to
your stature ? He himself will give you your garment.
His disciples say unto him, When wilt thou be manifest
to us, and when shall we see thee ? He saith, When ye
shall be stripped and not be ashamed . . .'

41–6. '. . . He said, The key of knowledge ye hid ; ye
entered not in yourselves and to them that were entering
in ye opened not.'

1–7. Cf. Matt. vi. 25 'Take no thought for your life, what
ye shall eat or what ye shall drink ; nor yet. for your body
what ye shall put on. Is not the life more than the food and
the body than the raiment ?', Luke xii. 22–3 ' Take no thought
for your life what ye shall eat ; nor yet for your body what ye
shall put on. For the life is more than the food, and the body
than the raiment.' The papyrus probably had the equivalent
of ' Take no thought ' at the beginning of the sentence, but
differs (1) by the addition of ' from morning . . . until morning,' (2) by the use of a different word for ' body ' and probably for ' life,' though it is possible that ' for your body ' or
' for your life ' preceded ' from morning ' in l. 1, (3) by the
omission of the second half of the Saying as recorded in the
Gospels.

7–13. Cf. Matt. vi. 28 (=Luke xii. 27) 'And why are ye
anxious concerning raiment ? Consider the lilies of the field,
how they grow ; they toil not, neither do they spin : yet I say
unto you that even Solomon in all his glory was not arrayed
like one of these,' and Matt. vi. 26 (=Luke xii. 4) ' Are ye
not of much more value than they (sc. the birds of heaven) ?'
The corresponding passage in the papyrus is not only much
shorter, but varies considerably, though to what extent is not
quite clear owing to the uncertainty attaching to the restoration of ll. 10–2.

13–5. Cf. Matt. vi. 27 (=Luke xii. 25) ' And which of you

by being anxious can add one cubit unto his stature?' The papyrus version is somewhat shorter, omitting 'by being anxious' and 'one cubit.' The position in which this Saying is found in the papyrus is also slightly different from that in the Gospels, where it immediately precedes instead of following the verse about the lilies.

15–6. Cf. Matt. vi. 31–3 'Be not therefore anxious, saying What shall we eat, or What shall we drink, or Wherewithal shall we be clothed? . . . for your heavenly Father knoweth that ye have need of all these things. But seek ye first his kingdom and his righteousness, and all these things shall be added unto you,' and Luke xii. 29–31, which is nearly identical and proceeds 'Fear not, little flock; for it is your Father's good pleasure to give you the kingdom.' The papyrus has the corresponding idea but expressed with extreme conciseness. 'He himself will give,' unless δώσει is an error for δώσω, raises a difficulty, for we should expect 'The Father will give' or 'God will give.' Apparently 'He himself' refers back to 'Father' or 'God' in the column preceding, or the author of the papyrus may have here incorporated from some source a Saying without its context which would have explained 'He himself.'

17–23. For the question cf. John xiv. 19 sqq. ' Yet a little while, and the world beholdeth me no more; but ye behold me : because I live ye shall live also. . . . Judas (not Iscariot) saith unto him, Lord, what is come to pass that thou wilt manifest thyself unto us and not unto the world?   Jesus answered . . . If a man love me, he will keep my word, and my Father will love him.' The answer ascribed in the papyrus to Jesus bears a striking resemblance to the answer made to a similar question in a passage of the Gospel according to the Egyptians which is referred to several times by Clement of Alexandria, and which ran thus : — 'When Salome asked how long death would prevail, the Lord said, So long as ye women bear children. For I have come to destroy the works of the female. And Salome said to him, Did I therefore well in bearing no children? The Lord answered and said, Eat every herb, but eat not that which has bitterness. When Salome asked when those things about which she questioned should be made known, the Lord said,

When ye trample upon the garment of shame; when the two
become one, and the male with the female neither male nor
female.' Cf. the Second Epistle of Clement xii. 2 (an early
Christian homily employing other Gospel materials besides the
Canonical Gospels) 'For the Lord himself being asked by some
one when his kingdom should come, said, When the two shall
be one, and the outside as the inside, and the male with the
female neither male nor female.' Both 'When ye shall be
stripped and not be ashamed' and 'When ye trample upon the
garment of shame' express the same idea, a mystical reference
to Gen. iii. 7, 'And they were both naked, the man and his wife,
and they were not ashamed,' the meaning in either case being
that Christ's kingdom on earth would not be manifested until
man had returned to the state of innocence which existed before
the Fall, and in which sexual ideas and relations had no place.
The chief differences between the two passages are (1) the setting, the questioner being in the Gospel according to the Egyptians Salome, and in the papyrus the disciples, (2) the simpler
language of the papyrus as contrasted with the more literary
and elaborated phrase 'trample upon the garment of shame,'
(3) the absence in the papyrus of the Ascetic tendency found
in the earlier part of the quotation from the Gospel according to the Egyptians. Whether the papyrus continued after
'ashamed' with something like 'and when the two become one
. . . ,' is of course uncertain, but Fr. (d), which probably belongs to the bottom of this column, is concerned with something different.

42–6. With the remains of these lines Dr. Bartlet compares
Luke xi. 52 'Woe unto you lawyers! for ye took away (Codex
Bezae and other MSS. 'ye hid') the key of knowledge; ye
entered not in yourselves and them that were entering in ye
hindered,' upon which passage our restorations are based. The
variant peculiar to the papyrus 'ye opened not' in place of 'ye
hindered' is a picturesque touch.

(*d*) GENERAL REMARKS.

This fragment (henceforth called 3) seems to belong to a
Gospel which was closely similar in point of form to the Synoptists.   The narrator speaks in the third person, not in the first,
and the portion preserved consists mainly of discourses which
are to a large extent parallel to passages in Matthew and Luke,
especially the latter Gospel, which alone seems to be connected
with ll. 41 sqq.   The papyrus version is, as a rule, shorter than
the corresponding passages in the Gospels; where it is longer
(ll. 1–3) the expansion does not alter the meaning in any way.
The chief interest lies in the question of the disciples and its
answer, both of which so closely correspond to a passage in
the Gospel according to the Egyptians and the uncanonical
Gospel or collection of Sayings used by the author of the
Second Epistle of Clement, that the Gospel of which 3 is a
fragment clearly belongs to the same sphere of thought.   Does
it actually belong to either of those works, which, though Harnack regards them as one and the same, are, we think, more
probably to be considered distinct?   In the Gospel according
to the Egyptians Salome was the questioner who occasioned
the remarkable Saying beginning, 'When ye trample upon
the garment of shame,' and it is much more likely that 3 presents a different version of the same incident in another Gospel,
than a repetition of the Salome question in a slightly different
form in another part of the Gospel according to the Egyptians.
Nor is 3 likely to be the actual Gospel which the author of the
Second Epistle of Clement was quoting.   It is unfortunate
that owing to the papyrus breaking off at 'ashamed' there is no
security that 'when the two become one,' or at any rate something very similar, did not follow, and the omission in the
Clement passage of a phrase corresponding to ll. 22–3 may be
a mere accident.   But the fact that the question in the Second
Epistle of Clement is worded somewhat differently, and is put
into the mouth of 'some one' instead of the disciples, as in 3,
is a good reason for rejecting the hypothesis that 3 is the Gospel quoted in the Epistle.

The evidence of 3 as to its origin being thus largely of a

negative character, we do not propose to discuss in detail
whether it is likely to belong to any of the other known Apocryphal Gospels. There are several to which it might be assigned, but direct evidence is wanting. If the Gospel according
to the Hebrews were thought of, it would be necessary to
suppose that the resemblances in 3 to Matthew and Luke did
not imply dependence upon them. In its relation to the Canonical Gospels 3 somewhat resembles the new Sayings, and
the view that 3 was, though no doubt at least secondary,
dependent not on Matthew and Luke, but upon some other
document, whether behind the Synoptists or merely parallel to
them, is tenable, but is less likely to commend itself to the
majority of critics than the opposite hypothesis that 3 is ultimately an abridgement of Matthew and Luke with considerable
alterations. In either case the freedom with which the author
of the papyrus Gospel handles the material grouped by St.
Matthew and St. Luke under the Sermon on the Mount is
remarkable. The Gospel from which 3 comes is likely to have
been composed in Egypt before A. D. 150, and to have stood
in intimate relation to the Gospel according to the Egyptians
and the uncanonical source used by the author of the Second
Epistle of Clement. Whether it was earlier or later than these
is not clear. The answer to the question put by the disciples
in 3 is couched in much simpler and clearer language than that
of the corresponding sentence in the answer to Salome, the
point of which is liable to be missed, while the meaning of 3.
22–3 is unmistakable. But the greater directness of the allu-
sion to Gen. iii. 7 in 3 can be explained either by supposing
that the version in the Gospel according to the Egyptians is
an Ascetic amplification of that in 3, or, almost but not quite
as well, in our opinion, by the view that the expression in 3 is
a toning down of the more striking phrase ' When ye trample
upon the garment of shame.'

There remains the question of the likelihood of a genuine
element in the story of which we now have three versions,
though how far these are independent of each other is uncertain. As is usual with uncanonical Sayings, the most diverse
opinions have been held about the two previously known pas-

sages. Previous criticism, which has recently tended to favour
the view that the story possesses at least a kernel of truth, is
now somewhat discounted by the circumstance that the phrase
' When ye trample upon the garment of shame ' has generally
been considered to mean ' when ye put off the body,' i. e. ' die,'
whereas the evidence of the parallel in the papyrus gives the
words a slightly different turn, and brings them more nearly
into line with the following sentences ' when the two become
one, &c.' But those critics would nevertheless seem in the
light of the new parallel to be right who maintain that the
passage in the Gospel according to the Egyptians does not go
much further in an Ascetic direction than e. g. Matt. xxii. 30
' For in the resurrection they neither marry nor are given in
marriage, but are as angels in heaven,' and Luke xx. 34–5
' The sons of this world marry and are given in marriage : but
they that are accounted worthy to attain to that world and the
resurrection from the dead neither marry nor are given in
marriage.' The occurrence of another version of the story is
an important additional piece of evidence in defence of the view
that it contains at least some elements of genuineness, and a
special interest attaches both to the form of the Saying in 3
on account of the clearness of its language, and to its context,
in which other matter closely related to the Canonical Gospels
is found in immediate proximity. All this lends fresh value to
what is, on account of the far-reaching problems connected
with it, one of the most important and remarkable, and, since
the discovery of 3, one of the better attested, of the Sayings
ascribed to our Lord outside the New Testament.